Sustainability
Micro Case Studies
for Food Processors

Working to Make a Better Tomorrow

David McGiverin & Pamela Barrow
Foreword by David Zepponi,
President, Northwest Food Processors
Association

Published by: Northwest Food Processors Association

ISBN: 1483932737
ISBN-13: 9781483932736

8338 NE Alderwood Road, Suite 160
Portland, Oregon 97220
http://www.nwfpa.org

Book Authors:
    David McGiverin, Northwest Food Processors Association
    Pamela Barrow, Northwest Food Processors Association

Contributors:
    Jennifer Ruwart, JR Collaborations
    Daniel Burgard, Cascade Earth Sciences

Cover Design: Marbry Walker, http://www.marbrywalker.com

Guidance:
    ConAgra Foods Lamb Weston (Paul Halberstadt)
    Del Monte Foods (Robin Connell & John Wisse)
    National Frozen Foods Corporation (Amyris Borgo)
    Oregon Cherry Growers, Inc. (Steve Kollars)
    J.R. Simplot Company (Alan Prouty)
    Tillamook County Creamery Association (Shawn Reiersgaard)
    Tree Top, Inc. (Chris Cary)
    Truitt Bros., Inc. (Heather McPherson)

This work was supported by a Specialty Crop Block Grant from the Idaho
Department of Agriculture and the Oregon Department of Agriculture. Some
materials are based upon work supported by the Hitachi Foundation.

For additional information, contact:
    sustainability@nwfpa.org
    503.327.2200
    http://www.nwfpa.org/sustainability

Contents:

Disclaimer

This book is designed to provide information and motivation to our readers. The content of each case study reflects the experience and the results of the reporting company. NWFPA and the publisher make no representations or warranties of any kind and assume no liabilities of any kind with respect to the application of the contents and specifically disclaim any fitness of use for a particular purpose or expected results. Neither NWFPA nor the publisher shall be responsible to any person or entity with respect to any loss or incidental or consequential damages caused or alleged to have been caused, directly or indirectly, by the information or actions contained herein. Every company is different and the ideas and strategies contained herein may not be suitable for your situation. You should seek the services of a competent professional before beginning any improvement program.

Forward

Sustainability is a topic of great importance to the food process-ing industry. Farmers are the original green industry—in a sense, the original sustainable industry. As part of the agricultural sys-tem, food processors are similarly humble and seldom tell the story of their commitment to sustainability. Yet their actions have benefited our communities, our workers, and the environment.

"Sustainability," with a capital "S," goes beyond simply sustain-ing a business over time, as many know; it includes growth in how we involve our businesses in society and within our natural environment. Within this book we find a compilation of stories that help all in our industry go beyond a focus on plant efficiency and profitability and beyond the deployment of capital and workforce. The case studies provided here will spark new ideas for improve-ment because they describe real changes that have been imple-mented by food companies that have experienced actual results. This book shows how companies have managed the complex theory of Sustainability by transforming knowledge into practice. It is a practical learning tool for the industry.

Contained within the front and back cover you will find a col-lection of original, brilliant, simple ideas that have helped many organizations reduce dependency on natural resources, create new innovative services, reduce costs, improve economics, and improve the quality of life of within their surrounding communities.

One company explains how they reduced solid waste to landfill by about 99% and realized over $860,000 in revenues by selling recovered materials. Another company shares how they reduced water use by 20,000 gallons per day with extraordinary return on investment.

The practices revealed here will not only help your business to become more sustainable but will build a more resilient and com-petitive industry. By implementing the practices described in this book, your effectiveness will be elevated to a new level, one that may have seemed impractical before.

In an increasingly globalized future, sustainability helps drive competitive advantage. Sustainability—as a theory or idea—has little to no value unless put into practice. That is why this book is so important. It is time for food processors to tell their story.

David Zepponi
President, Northwest Food Processors Association

Introduction

Although there are many definitions of sustainability, sustainability has become the catchword of the decade. Over time, it has evolved from a mere catchword to a business concept that is being embraced by more and more companies and that is seen as increasing profitability while at the same time reducing environmental impacts and enhancing social responsibility.

Many companies are developing sustainability programs to guide their sustainability efforts. A robust sustainability program can be thought of as a three-legged stool, with environmental (planet), economic (profit) and social (people) issues each representing a leg of the stool. These three legs are often referred to as the "triple bottom line."

The environmental leg represents efforts to balance the use of limited resources today with the resource needs of tomorrow. Environmental sustainability addresses such topics as energy, water use, invasive species, genetically modified seeds, chemical fertilizers, soil erosion, and the preservation of farmland.

The economic sustainability leg of the stool focuses on issues which allow business to thrive in both the community and the marketplace. Economic sustainability initiatives return a profit to shareholders or cooperative members, develop value-added products, establish market share, eliminate artificial barriers to business, and work to establish a level playing field in the marketplace.

The third leg, social responsibility, involves a company's role in supporting a healthy and secure workforce and investing in the community through taxes, leadership, social justice, and philanthropy.

In 2010 the Northwest Food Processors Association (NWFPA) adopted the 1987 Brundtland Commission definition of Sustainability that states:

> *Sustainable development is development that meets the needs of the present without compromising the ability of future generations to meet their own needs.*

Based on this foundational definition, NWFPA set its objective to "mainstream sustainability in the food processing industry" and help food processors incorporate sustainability into their business practices. To further this objective, NWFPA is creating frameworks, guidance, and resources that food processors can use in developing individual company sustainability programs and plans.

NWFPA developed this book as a vehicle for food processors to share real life sustainability practices and actions they are taking to become more sustainable. It is also designed to be a catalyst to inspire companies to take action and adopt new and better ways of doing business. The intent is that readers will identify ideas and actions that they can modify and implement in their own facilities.

The book is divided into three sections and each section addresses one of the three legs of sustainability: *social sustainability*, *environmental sustainability*, and *economic sustainability*. Each section begins with a definition and an introduction explaining the elements of the individual "leg." The body of the section presents the various practices, actions or approaches that were submitted by individual companies.

Food processors have a long history of finding ways to become more sustainable and they value continuous improvements to these efforts. Processors realize that sustainability is good for both the environment and long-term economic viability.

These values are best expressed through the Northwest Food Processors Association's Sustainability Statement:

> *The food processing industry has been, and continues to be, an integral part of the Northwest economy for over a century. Continued viability of our industry will be dependent on the success of our ongoing efforts to address water, energy, safety, community, and environmental responsibilities.*

> *—Northwest Food Processors Association*
> *Sustainability Task Force, 2010*

The question for food processors today is not *if*, but *how* they should manage their sustainability activities.

Note: This publication is the first edition of the Sustainability Micro Case Studies. NWFPA will be collecting additional case studies to include in an expanded second edition. If your company is engaging in sustainable practices, NWFPA would like to hear from you so that we can share your practices with other food processors. Information on preparing and submitting your case studies to NWFPA can be found on the following page.

Share Your Story!

Please tell us about your company's sustainable practices so we can include them in the next edition of this book and recognize your efforts.

Use the following format:

1. **Project Description/Title: Provide name of project.**

2. **Existing Conditions: What prompted your company to move ahead with the project? What motivated action?**

3. **Project Detail:**

   a. **Provide a brief summary of the activities that were performed and where in the operation they were performed to reduce water usage or become more efficient.**

   b. **Identify measurements (metrics) used to determine the effect and success of the project.**

4. **Considerations, Challenges, and Obstacles: Were there any foreseen or unforeseen setbacks that your company needed to overcome? Briefly describe.**

5. **Sustainable Features: How does the project support and/or contribute to social, economic, and environmental sustainability?**

6. **Quantifiable Benefits: Provide resulting benefits such as water volumes reduced, energy savings, cost**

savings, and/or return on investment, such as reduced O&M, chemical usage, etc.).

7. **Additional Resources:** Consultants, web sites, organizations and other information sources that helped you with the project.

Submit practices to: sustainability@nwfpa.org

If you have questions or need assistance, please contact NWFPA at 503-327-2200 or sustainability@nwfpa.org

ABOUT NORTHWEST FOOD PROCESSORS ASSOCIATION

Formed in 1914, and headquartered in Portland, Oregon, the Northwest Food Processors Association (NWFPA) serves as an advocate for the interests of its members and as a resource for enhancing their competitive capabilities. NWFPA's membership includes national companies with facilities in the Pacific Northwest, regional companies and locally run businesses. NWFPA is one of the largest food processing trade associations, with current membership of more than 125 food processor companies with over 220 facilities and more than 370 supplier members. Primary members are located in the states of Idaho, Oregon and Washington; with affiliate members located outside the Northwest and in Canada.

NWFPA focuses its efforts on policy, technical, regulatory and advocacy in the major issues impacting the food processing industry: Energy, Environmental, Government Affairs, Operations & Technical Affairs, Sustainability and Workforce Productivity. Processor members provide advice and guide association activities and priorities through participation in committees and task forces in these issue areas. NWFPA is governed by a board of directors elected by the membership.

NWFPA delivers information, training, tools and resources on important matters affecting the food processing industry. A primary vehicle is the annual Northwest Food Manufacturing & Packaging Exposition and Conference. Held in January, it is the largest regional food manufacturing tradeshow in North America and attracts about 4000 food processing industry professionals from across the country. In addition to featuring over 425 exhibitor booths, the event offers a comprehensive program of leading-edge educational sessions.

Events specifically related to sustainability include the annual Sustainability Summit, held in Portland in mid-April and the annual NW Industrial Energy Efficiency Summit co-located with the Exposition and Conference. The Sustainability Summit brings together food processors, sustainability experts and industry partners working to advance sustainability in the food processing industry. Sessions are focused on practical industrial applications of sustainability management practices. For information see **www.nwfpa.org/sustainabilitysummit.**

The NW Industrial Energy Efficiency Summit, produced by NWFPA in conjunction with the Northwest's major energy organizations, is the region's premier gathering of industries and energy interests working to advance industrial competitiveness through energy efficiency. Sessions focus on practical applications of energy efficient technologies in both electricity and natural gas and energy management approaches with energy experts and industry personnel presenting real-life energy savings success stories and challenges. The Energy Summit is now in its sixth year. For information see **www.nwfpa.org/energysummit.**

For additional information about NWFPA, educational resources, events, or membership, see www.nwfpa.org or contact:

info@nwfpa.orgor call **503-327-2200.**

NWFPA SUSTAINABILITY PROGRAM

Northwest Food Processors Association (NWFPA) leadership identified Sustainability as a key strategic priority for the food processing industry. NWFPA's sustainability efforts began with the formation of a Sustainability Task Force charged with defining sustainability from a food industry perspective, guiding the development of a framework and identifying resources necessary to help mainstream sustainability throughout the region's food processing industry.

In 2010, NWFPA adopted the following widely accepted definition of sustainability:

Sustainable development is development that meets the needs of the present without compromising the ability of future generations to meet their own needs.

(Bruntland Commission 1987)

In 2012, NWFPA launched a major sustainability initiative and the NWFPA board of directors elevated the Sustainability Task Force to standing committee status in the association. The new Sustainability Committee's membership was broadened to include representatives of NWFPA's five other standing committees. This echoes the contemporary approach to sustainability as the umbrella under which many areas of effort fall, including energy, water, waste, greenhouse gas emissions, workforce, and community involvement. Broader participation assures development of products and services that will provide resources for NWFPA members in their sustainability efforts.

SUSTAINABILITY FACTORS

The NWFPA Task Force identified the following as important factors to be considered in developing and implementing a sustainability program:

- Continuous availability of resources including water, land and energy products at sustainable levels, quality and cost;
- Acknowledgement of sustainability as a factor in consumer purchasing preferences; positive business and brand recognition associated with our products which are recognized as sustainable by consumers;
- Implementing sustainability is challenging and complex, especially measurement and reporting and supply chain effects;
- Importance of participating in public, legislative and regulatory arenas that can impact or influence sustainable practices;
- Sustainability performance can impact the ability of employers to attract and maintain high-performing talent; and

- Honest reporting and communications on sustainability efforts.

SUSTAINABILITY RESOURCES

The following resources are available for download on the NWFPA web site at **www.nwfpa.org** and their development was funded by a Specialty Crop Block Grant from the Oregon

Department of Agriculture and the Idaho Department of Agriculture:

- ***Sustainability Guide*** — provides a resource that assists companies in the development of an individualized sustainability program to meet the needs of their companies, their communities and their consumers.
- ***Water Sustainability Training Course*** — provides three training modules to educate food processing personnel about the importance of water sustainability and the activities that are performed to achieve efficient water use.
- ***Sustainability Micro Case Studies for Food Processors*** — presents real-life sustainability actions and approaches that are designed to provide ideas for sustainability efforts and to inspire others to apply in their own organizations.
- ***NWFPA's Energy Roadmap for Members*** charts a suggested path for individual food processors to achieve energy intensity reductions. Food processors can use the Roadmap as a guide for setting energy intensity goals and for developing a strategic energy management plan or action plan for their facilities. It also includes a self-assessment to help companies gauge their current level

of energy efficiency efforts and identify actions that could allow them to operate at a higher level of efficiency. The appendices include supporting information as well as valuable resource contacts. The Roadmap is publicly available on NWFPA's web site for download at **www.nwfpa.org/energy**

Visit the Sustainability pages on the NWFPA web site at www.nwfpa.org to obtain downloadable versions of sustainability resources for the food processing industry.

NWFPA's online resource, the Food Resources & Education Institute, or FREDi, provides information, white papers, training, event calendar, and networking opportunities that can provide additional help for food processors in all areas of sustainability. FREDi can be accessed at **www.fredtalks.com**

SECTION ONE

SOCIAL SUSTAINABILITY

Social Sustainability is the positive effect that a company has on society through community investment. This includes providing safe and nutritious food, safe jobs, and community development."

—Northwest Food Processors Sustainability Guide

INTRODUCING SOCIAL SUSTAINABILITY

In the Northwest, the food processing industry has a significant influence on the economic health of surrounding communities, especially in rural areas. Key economic activities associated with food processing include the farming, harvesting, processing, and distribution of agricultural and natural resource products. These activities provide direct and indirect employment as well as opportunities for people to engage in community services. Employees serve as volunteer firefighters, Little League coaches, teacher assistants, choir members, and scout leaders. A company that understands its ties to a community promotes a vibrant workforce when it provides employees opportunities to give back to the community. This relationship among the company, its employees, and the community instills trust, pride, and loyalty. Bright futures for a company and its community are inextricably intertwined.

Quality of life is important for employee and community well-being. A living-wage job with opportunities for personal development and employee engagement within a safe and supportive environment are essential for good morale. Happy employees take pride in what they do, are healthier, and have good social relationships—and this spirit spills over into the entire community.

Food safety is a major public concern and is a priority of food processors. It is the "product responsibility" of the food processing industry, and poorly handled prevention and response can erode trust in a company's products. USDA and FDA regulations are extremely complex, and companies direct significant resources toward compliance. Support of research on better and quicker pathogen detection methods and new and safer processing and packaging will promote greater safety and consumer trust in the industry.

Community outreach demonstrates a company's vested interest in its community. Outreach efforts include partnering with community programs like community cleanup, charitable giving, or empowering those in need, providing vocational educational opportunities like internships, apprenticeships, or tours for schools, and delivering general skills training for employees, such as learning a new language, health/safety certifications, or technology courses. These can be achieved by offering incentives and/or time for employees to pursue their passions, while providing forums for employees to share ideas and work together.

Questions to Ask

- What is your company doing to engage and empower employees?
- Do employees at your company have opportunities to learn and grow?
- What values/interests/passions does your company share with the local community?

- What role can your company play in the local community?
- Do you have programs to encourage employee volunteerism?

Life Skills Training for Immigrant Workers Benefits Employees and Employer

Bellingham Cold Storage

OPPORTUNITY

Gayle Davis teaches English to immigrant employees at Bellingham Cold Storage (BCS). She noticed that her students faced many challenges in being new to the United States besides language that impacted their ability to perform at full potential.

SOLUTION

Employees now learn the basics of living in the United States as part of their English classes, including how to use US currency, shop for familiar foods and necessities, communicate with families back home, and navigate situational experiences, such as attending a child's parent-teacher conference.

RESULTS

Since adding life skills to the English classes to help employees overcome personal issues, BCS has seen increased employee morale and Improved employee health. There have also been positive outcomes for the company including increased quality and production, and reduced absenteeism and turnover.

The program also creates a strong internal labor pool for recruiting and promoting, and a robust employee referral pipeline because employees feel valued and cared for. The company gains a reputation as a great place to work, attracting the best talent in the area.

On-Site Health Clinic Improves Employee Health and Reduces Health Care Costs

Bellingham Cold Storage

OPPORTUNITY

In the mid-2000s Bellingham Cold Storage (BCS) became a self-insured company, saving the company $400,000 to $600,000 annually. Even with this dramatic cost savings, BCS still wondered how it might better manage its health care costs while improving the overall health of its employees.

A cost analysis indicated that it may be more cost-efficient for BCS to run its own on-site clinic. This could also address many of the barriers to care that increase use of emergency care:

- Availability of appointments
- Location of services
- Finding a trusted health-care provider
- Co-pays that felt prohibitively high

SOLUTION

BCS decided to proceed with an on-site clinic. Since BCS itself did not have enough potential patients to make a clinic viable, it invited one of its tenants, Trans-Ocean Products, to become a partner in the health care clinic, called the MiCare Clinic.

Now, employees of both companies have access to on-site, high-quality, personalized care at no cost. Employees and their dependents can make 20-minute appointments with no waiting and no co-pay. The clinic's pharmacy stocks over 100 medications, which are provided to patients also without co-pay for the first 90 days of a prescription.

RESULTS

Both BCS and Trans-Ocean Products say that it is too early to tell but are confident they will see healthier employees and lower costs. Because employees primarily access care when they are sick, BCS and Trans-Ocean are exploring incentives to encourage employees to focus on preventative medicine.

Voluntary Full Safety Compliance Reduces Injuries and Premiums

Henningsen Cold Storage

OPPORTUNITY

Henningsen Cold Storage (HCS) employees work in extreme temperatures, performing heavy-duty labor.

The company knows that injuries not only impact productivity but also impact employees' quality of life. HCS wanted a program that would help the company and its workers minimize on-the-job hazards and prevent injuries, illnesses, and deaths in the workplace.

SOLUTION

Rather than wait for the Occupational Safety and Health Administration (OSHA) to conduct an on-site inspection, which are conducted randomly and without advance notice, HCS sought OSHA's assistance to bring the company into full compliance with OSHA requirements.

RESULTS

Company leaders have made safety a daily way of doing business at HCS. Each individual location and location manager is responsible for the facility safety plan. The managers , direct reports, and safety committee execute the safety plan and all employees are actively engaged in safety. As a result of this and other practices HCS has implemented, its Experience Modification Factor(MOD) rate is .80, which is one of the lowest in the industry. In addition to fewer accidents, insurance claims have been reduced, premiums reduced, and employee satisfaction and morale has increased.

Horn Honking Reduces Fork-Lift Accidents

Henningsen Cold Storage

OPPORTUNITY

At any given time, Henningsen Cold Storage (HCS) has multiple forklift drivers driving pallets to and from the dock, entering and leaving its warehouses, and loading and unloading pallets from cold storage. With multiple blind spots and a demanding schedule, there are ample opportunities for accidents and collisions with pedestrians. HCS sought a simple yet effective method for reducing forklift accidents.

SOLUTION

To warn people of a possible danger, drivers honk before entering and leaving the warehouses, before making sharp turns and when pedestrians are on the road or in the aisles.

RESULTS

The simple honking of a horn makes both drivers and pedestrians more conscious of their surroundings and potential dangers, and has lead to a decrease in the number of on-the-job accidents and injuries. This in turn reduces insurance claims and premiums.

Create a Formal Process to Recognize Employees' Efforts

Green Mountain Coffee Roasters, Inc.

OPPORTUNITY

Green Mountain Coffee Roasters has a reputation as a great employer and overall employee satisfaction is consistently high. However, an annual employee survey revealed dissatisfaction with company acknowledgement and celebration of personal and professional milestones. Green Mountain desired to create a more formal process for celebrating milestones, from birthdays and employment anniversaries to the successful completion of projects, such as a software implementation.

SOLUTION

The monthly employee newsletter now includes employee birthdays and employment anniversaries, and it acknowledges employees for reaching their goals.

RESULTS

Employee recognition and celebration of personal milestones has created camaraderie among employees and goodwill between Green Mountain and its employees. It has also increased employees' personal pride in contribution and driven friendly competition as employees know that delivering superior results will be recognized.

Cultivate Managers and Leaders by Providing Educational Opportunities

Henningsen Cold Storage

OPPORTUNITY

Henningsen Cold Storage (HCS) operates in an industry with an average turnover rate of 35%. High turnover drives up recruitment and on-boarding costs and can make it challenging to cultivate an internal labor force for promotions and advancements.

HCS addressed high turnover by creating a culture where managers "hire to fit" by asking *"Will this person fit within our group?"* Managers strive to *hire* for customer service and attitude and then to *train* in specific skills. Once the right candidates were hired, HCS sought further opportunities for managers to identify and cultivate frontline workers for supervisory and manager positions.

SOLUTION

Managers nominate employees to attend the WFLO Institute, which is an arm of the World Food Logistics Organization. If approved by the executive team, these employees attend three days of in-depth classes in cold storage, or public refrigerated warehousing, annually for three consecutive years. Employees are selected based on the following characteristics: productivity, leadership, willingness to take on increasing levels of responsibility, strong communication skills, respect and likability by management and the team, and a "make it happen" attitude.

RESULTS

The WFLO training opportunities have improved employee satisfaction, loyalty, and morale and have expanded the skills of HCS employees, increasing productivity and improving customer service.

Photo ID Badges Personalize the Workplace

Dave's Killer Bread

OPPORTUNITY

As Dave's Killer Bread grew, it became increasingly difficult for managers and leaders to remember the names of all employees. The company needed a way to help managers learn and remember the names of frontline workers as part of a continuing effort to encourage authentic connections between managers and employees.

SOLUTION

All employees now wear photo ID badges.

RESULTS

Wearing photo ID badges has made employees feel *seen*. The quality of their work has tended to improve, as they also feel more accountable. Employees also feel more valued when managers know who they are and take an interest in their work and their lives. They take more pride in their work, which has had a positive impact on productivity.

Training for Special Needs Individuals Produces Skilled and Dedicated Workers

Tim's Cascade Snacks

OPPORTUNITY

Tim's Cascade Snacks (Tim's) has been manufacturing unique potato chips and other snacks since 1986 using an old family recipe. Tim's has created a loyal and dedicated workforce through its numerous community support and outreach efforts. The company wanted a way to provide employment to the underserved and those with various disabilities.

SOLUTION

Tim's works closely with its community partners Auburn School District and Vadis Northwest to provide employment opportunities to special education students and individuals with mental, physical, or developmental disabilities. The company currently employs three trainees: one from Auburn and two from Vadis, though these numbers change from year to year.

RESULTS

The company believes that these individuals deserve a chance to earn a living wage and has experienced that they often become extremely dedicated and dependable employees. When feasible, Tim's transitions the trainees into permanent positions.

Partnership with Oregon Food Bank Drives Hunger Relief

Pacific Natural Foods and Oregon Food Bank Partnership

OPPORTUNITY

In pursuit of its core belief that no person should be hungry, Pacific Natural Foods donates to the Oregon Food Bank (OFB). But the company wanted to increase OFB services to the disadvantaged by allowing OFB to accept food and agricultural donations that otherwise could not be distributed through the OFB Network.

SOLUTION

Pacific Natural Foods developed a unique and multifaceted partnership with OFB. The company donates countless hours of production line time, labor, R&D, ingredients, and packaging to

OFB. In addition, Pacific Natural Foods encourages participation and engagement through the following programs:

- Employees volunteer at the Oregon Food Bank
- Customers encouraged to aid in hunger relief. Pacific Natural product labels express the company's commitment and encourage customers to follow its lead
- Employees giving campaign to OFB.

RESULTS

Over the past 10 years, Pacific Natural Foods has donated more than 9.4 million pounds of food to the Oregon Food Bank. In fiscal year 2011, Pacific Natural Foods donated 1.2 million pounds of food, which is equivalent to 923,077 meals.

PART TWO

ENVIRONMENTAL SUSTAINABILITY

Environmental Sustainability is availability of resources including water, land, and energy to grow and process food products at sustainable rates, quality, and cost through continuous improvement.

—Northwest Food Processors Sustainability Guide

INTRODUCING ENVIRONMENTAL SUSTAINABILITY

Food production practices can potentially have profound impacts on an ecosystem and its natural resources. The way we cultivate crops, redistribute water, and dispose of waste can mean the difference between a thriving wetlands and a desolate landscape. Through our raw products, food processors are directly linked to the natural environment. Responsible stewardship of the environment is critical to a sustained food processing industry.

Land provides the substance from which our food sources derive sustenance and grow. It is the foundation of the food industry. Unsustainable practices can lead to encroachment of invasive species, degradation of soil nutrients, and over-reliance on fertilizers and pesticides. The long-term viability of the food processing industry is dependent on healthy land resources.

Water is the lifeblood of the environment, providing a constant stream of sustenance that can enhance or limit a region's ability to survive. Water is a critical input to agriculture and food processing, and many of the larger food processors use over a million gallons of water per day. But water supply and availability are becoming significant concerns in parts of the Northwest as well as the nation. Industrial wastewater is also an important environmental concern. To assure that sufficient clean water is available for our and future generations, water must be efficiently used and wastewater properly treated and disposed.

Waste and Emissions are of particular concern as new food safety standards have demanded sanitary packaging and containers that when disposed of can present a significant burden to the environment. Today's processed goods are often individually wrapped, placed in lined retail packages, boxed for transport, and then placed on pallets or crates. This produces a substantial amount of solid waste that ends up in landfills and creates pollution.

Energy is needed to fuel farm equipment and run irrigation pumps, to run food processing and packaging equipment, and to transport goods to market. Food processing is an energy-intensive industry and is the second-largest industrial user of electricity in the Northwest. In addition, energy generation and fossil fuel use account for the vast majority of greenhouse gas emissions.

Questions to Ask

1. Does my company have policies and goals in place to manage our use of natural resources?
2. Does my company have reduction or efficiency goals for water, waste, and energy?
3. What types of waste does my company produce?
4. What are my suppliers doing to reduce waste or use resources more efficiently?
5. Can my company partner with nearby companies to reduce waste or increase efficiencies?

Automatic Flow Controls Save Water and Reduce Costs

Seneca Foods Corporation

OPPORTUNITY

The water supply for the flumes that convey product to processing equipment used to be manually regulated at Seneca Foods Corporation. Frequently, the flow to the flumes would exceed the flume capacity and water would spill onto the floor and down the drain. Seneca Foods spent time observing and measuring the overflow rate and determined that the wasted water averaged 36,000 gallons per day (25 gallons per minute).

SOLUTION

The water supply flow was automated by adding a float to control an Asco brand valve on the input line. This simple modification automatically controlled the flow to the amount of water necessary to keep the flumes operating efficiently with no wasted water.

RESULTS

The capital cost was approximately $1,500 to reduce water consumption and discharge by 1.8 million gallons per year during the 50-day operating period. Total savings on the combined cost of water supply and treatment was $6,842 per year.

Comprehensive Assessment and Plan Reduce Water Use by 24%

ConAgra Foods Lamb Weston

OPPORTUNITY

ConAgra Foods Lamb Weston sought to significantly reduce water use at one of its plants.

SOLUTION

The company conducted a comprehensive review of all plant water systems and piping and developed a cost-effective plan to reduce water use.

Plant teams from across the organization—engineers, area and team leads, managers, and maintenance personnel—were assigned to one or more of 28 areas within the plant. Each team identified water lines running through the plant, measured flow, and then verified and corrected existing piping drawings.

RESULTS

Collection of facility-wide water-use data led to the identification and implementation of 16 measures and 31 preventative maintenance items to reduce daily water use per pound of product by an average of 24%. In addition to implemented measures and items, the plant teams also identified further water use reduction opportunities.

Screen Solids and Use Low-Flow Spray Bars to Reduce Wastewater Costs

Del Monte Foods

OPPORTUNITY

Solids in the company's wastewater were high and extra fees were being paid to treat them. After reviewing options for removing the solids, Del Monte Foods determined that reducing the amounts of solids introduced into the water and improved screening would be the simplest options.

SOLUTION

A Lyco brand rotary screen was installed in the waste pit to screen solids out of the water prior to discharge. In addition, solid gutter plates were installed to help reduce the amount of large solids entering the wastewater stream and to make the screens work better.

While looking for ways to reduce water use, the company noticed that the water used in the preparation department could be reduced without affecting product quality. Water flow was reduced through installation of a filtered low-flow spray bar system throughout the preparation department. The filtration before the spray bar was important for preventing the spray nozzles from plugging.

RESULTS

This project reduced water consumption by 20,000 gallons per day as well as saving over $25,000 annually

Low Capital and Behavioral Changes Reduce Wastewater Discharges by 19%

ConAgra Foods Lamb Weston

OPPORTUNITY

A ConAgra Foods Lamb Weston vegetable plant sought to reduce its wastewater discharge.

SOLUTION

A thorough water-usage review helped the ConAgra team identify conservation opportunities in several areas: Installing flow-restrictive devices and automatic-control valves for chill-system sprays, re-plumbing recycled process water for receiving wash water, and reducing freeze-tunnel defrost times as well as process water filter backwash cycles.

Further water savings measures included eliminating continual belt washing, chill room gutter-flushing, and the removal of a wash tank in carrot receiving.

Operating and maintenance personnel were engaged in sustaining the reductions through awareness education activities and daily use tracking.

RESULTS

The vegetable plant reduced wastewater discharge by 19% per pound of product during the six-month growing season via low-capital, high-awareness conservation efforts.

Rejuvenate Engineered Wetlands for More Effective Nutrient Recycling

ConAgra Foods Lamb Weston

OPPORTUNITY

Engineered wetlands were installed 17 years ago at this ConAgra Foods Lamb Weston location. The wetlands filter nutrient-dense wastewater prior to application on suitable land and crops. The company conducted the first major restoration of engineered wetlands at this location. This will ensure the continued protection of critical groundwater areas.

SOLUTION

Lamb Weston revitalized the process water treatment system to original design levels. The company restored five of the twelve wetland cells in its engineered water treatment system for this location. Restoration included removal of decaying plant vegetation, removal and recycling of sludge/debris from ponds, and transplanting vigorous cattails from other ponds.

RESULTS

In addition to more effective water-to-soil nutrient recycling, the wetland rejuvenation restored pond water flow and dispersion as well as open-water habitats.

Re-piping and Water Recycling Reduces Water Use and Energy Costs

ConAgra Foods Lamb Weston

OPPORTUNITY

Boiler operators are required to sample and monitor boiler water several times a day to assure its quality. When sampling, Lamb Weston operators noticed that a large amount of water was being wasted during the process. They wanted to develop a new system for more efficient water travel and for water recovery.

SOLUTION

Revise the piping system for sampling and allow the reuse of large volumes of reverse osmosis water.

RESULT

A 15% reduction in wasted water was realized. Another environmental and economic benefit was the reduction of heating inputs. The boiler water was recycled back to the storage tank at an already warm temperature, resulting in less energy needed to heat the water for the boiler.

Automatic Solenoid Valves Assure Water Used Only When Needed

YoCream International, Inc./ The Dannon Company, Inc.

OPPORTUNITY

YoCream manufactures frozen yogurt and frozen beverages for the foodservice industry. Containers are filled with yogurt using a machine on the production line called a carton filler. As cartons exit the filler, they are sprayed with a stream of water to ensure there is no yogurt on the outside of the carton. Historically, these spray nozzles had to be turned off manually at the end of the day or anytime there were no cartons going through the filler. During any technical downtime, the water continued to pour all over the conveyor belt and down the drain. YoCream wanted a way to ensure that water was sprayed only when cartons were going through the filler.

SOLUTION

Install solenoid valves with automation that turns the water on only if the carton infeed is engaged. This ensures the production line only uses water when needed. No extra sensors or equipment had to be installed other than the valves.

RESULTS

YoCream was able to save about 360 gallons of water per day.

Water Use Reduction and Wasted Product Recovery

Western Polymer Corporation

OPPORTUNITY

To produce modified potato starch for the paper industry, Western Polymer relies on groundwater from an aquifer that is overused and declining. The company desired to reduce its freshwater use and reliance on the aquifer.

SOLUTION

In 2002, the company started working to reduce fresh water usage by making changes to its starch cleaning system. In 2006, Western Polymer installed more water-efficient starch cleaning equipment that further reduced water usage. In early 2007, a recovery tank was added, allowing water to be recycled before it is released to land application.

RESULTS

Changes to the cleaning system have reduced both wastewater and solid waste discharges. Wastewater discharge was reduced 64% from 2002 to 2006, with a reduction of 88% for 2007. Solid waste (starch residue) was reduced 85% from 2005; the remaining 15% is now being used for agricultural feed.

Savings from the 619,650 to 729,000 pounds starch per year not discharged as waste has been over $100,000 per year from an investment of approximately $85,000. The changes also reduced the consumption and discharge of more than 290,400 pounds of cationic reagent with the wastewater and wasted starch. Fresh-water consumption was reduced by 15,676,000 gallons in 2006 compared to 2002 and another 5,790,000 gallons in 2007, for a total reduction of 21,466,000 gallons per year.

Boiler Piping Improvements Reduce Water and Energy Consumption

Pacific Pure-Aid Company

OPPORTUNITY

Pacific Pure-Aid Company uses steam from a boiler to extract moisture from its fruit and vegetable products to between a 1 and 5% ratio on the surface of their dryer drums. Heating approximately 9,200 gallons of water five to seven days a week, 24 hours a day, from 35 degrees to over 212 degrees to produce this steam used a lot of energy. The company wanted to implement enhancements to the boiler condensate system for the double drum dryers. Areas looked at for better energy efficiency included the amount of water being used to operate the boilers, the amount of water that was being discharged into the sanitary system, and also the cold temperature of the water supply.

SOLUTION

Pacific Pure-Aid partnered with its boiler chemical provider and boiler service company to develop a condensate return system with more energy-efficient plumbing, components, and boiler feed water control. Savings were realized by installing new piping and insulating lines and adding a modulating control value. A continuous loop system for the heated returned condensate now allows reuse of water.

RESULTS

This new system not only reduced water and energy use, but the consistent temperature allows better equipment performance for quicker processing, easier use of the dryers, and a more uniform temperature of the dehydrating surface for a more consistent finished product. The new system also reduced the amount of chemicals needed to maintain the boiler condition.

Bill Cummins, plant engineer, verified the efficiency of the new system by comparing 24- to 48-hour runs on identical products. Daily reports by plant maintenance personnel documented an 85% reduction in water use by the boiler. NW Natural Gas provided daily reports, via email, showing therms used per hour that indicated a 20% reduction in natural gas use. The return on investment, primarily from energy savings, boiler feed water consumption reduction, and reduced boiler chemical use, was seven months on a cost of $35,280.

Onsite Waste Water Treatment and Biogas Recovery Reduce Sewer Fees and Energy Costs

Sierra Nevada Brewing Co.

OPPORTUNITY

Brewery effluent water is typically very high in organic solids and requires more treatment than a typical residential effluent stream. As brewery production increased, so did Sierra Nevada Brewing Co.'s impact on the local municipal water treatment system.

SOLUTION

To reduce impact, the brewery installed an onsite wastewater treatment facility in 2002 to pretreat all of its brewing process water. Vaults around the brewery collect process water for treatment and reuse. The water is separated from any remaining spent grain, which is sent to an onsite composter. An equalization tank ensures that the water is the appropriate temperature and pH. The water then moves into an anaerobic digester that produces methane-rich biogas. A recovery system captures this gas, cleans it up a bit, and sends it to fuel Sierra Nevada's boilers to offset the natural gas needed to run the system. Following the anaerobic digestion phase, water is further treated in an aeration basin to remove biological compounds before finishing in clarifying basins to settle out remaining solids.

RESULTS

Sierra Nevada's treatment plant sends water roughly equivalent to residential effluent water composition to the municipal plant instead of water with a high solids content typical of a brewery. The treatment process eliminates roughly 90% of the loading in the water. Additionally, the biogas produced at the anaerobic digester can be burned in place of natural gas in the company's boilers. Sierra Nevada's water treatment system significantly reduces its impact on the municipal system, reduces sewer fees, and provides free fuel for its boilers. This project is expected to pay for itself in roughly five to six years.

Reduced Water Use, Discharge and Solids Decrease Water Costs and Wastewater Fees

Quincy Foods, Inc.

OPPORTUNITY

Quincy Foods discharges wastewater to the City of Quincy Industrial Wastewater Treatment Plant (Quincy IWWTP). Discharge costs from the City are based 50% on flow and 50% on load in the water.

The Quincy Foods wastewater discharge was at or near the limit of 2.2 million gallons per day on a regular basis, and fees were high. In addition, the Quincy IWWTP was near its capacity and needed additional capacity for new industrial users. Reduced flows would save money, reduce water use, and help minimize future costs for expansion of the Quincy IWWTP, which would be shared by all dischargers.

SOLUTION

Quincy Foods staff made it a priority to reduce water use and created a two-phase project: Phase 1 would reduce water use and discharge volume and Phase 2 would reduce the load of biochemical oxygen demand (BOD) and total suspended solids (TSS). Phase 1 was implemented in steps:

Step 1: The most appropriate measurement for water use reduction was determined: gallons of water use per pound of finished product.

Step 2: All pipes, valves, and fittings were inspected, and leaks were identified and fixed.

Step 3: Better flow data was collected. Flow meters were placed on water supply lines to specific water use areas or equipment where possible, one line at a time. Hourly water use data was collected to correlate with processing activities.

Step 4: Data was reviewed, and associates got out on the floor to determine why and how the water use varied and what practices used the most water.

Step 5: Solutions and ideas for controlling water use and reusing water were tested and implemented:

- Fixed water leaks.
- Put spray nozzles with automatic shutoffs on open hoses.
- Revised cleaning practices to use less water by using foam and brushes to first loosen grime and debris and

then lightly hose off, instead of cleaning everything with high-pressure water.

- Reduced or eliminated the use of high-pressure water.
- Installed a screen to clean post-blancher chiller water and reused the chiller water to supplement the pre-blanch wash water.
- Revised blancher operations to reduce operating water levels and overflows to the minimum needed to maintain adequate quality with minimum water use.

In implementing the project, it was important to narrow down the project to workable steps to help determine the where, how, why, and what of changing water use. A majority of the effort was educational. Antiquated practices and habits required effort to re-train experienced operators into a new way of thinking. Changes to the practices required experimentation and testing to find out how much water reduction was appropriate and how much was too much.

RESULTS

Water use was reduced by half from 1.5 to 2 gallons of water per pound of product to 0.8 to 0.9 gallons per pound of product. The investment in Phase 1 entailed flow meters, automatic shut-off spray nozzles, repairs to leaks, a screen with tank, new piping for chiller water reuse, and employee training. The investment was minimal, and the return on the investment came as reduced water supply cost and reduced wastewater fees. In addition, energy costs were substantially reduced by improved blancher operations because less water was required to be heated and reduced water pressure was needed for cleanup.

The benefits of reduced water use are community-wide. The reduction in flow by Quincy Foods and the other local major food processor has allowed the Quincy IWWTP to accept cooling water from the local computer data center users who were discharging to the municipal wastewater treatment plant. The municipal wastewater treatment plant improved without the "clean" cooling water diluting its treatment, and the result is more reliable treatment to high-quality reclaimed wastewater for groundwater recharge. The reduced water use and groundwater recharge helps improve the long-term sustainability of the local groundwater aquifer, which has been declining.

Sustainable Farming Practices, Solar Power, Recycling and Rail

Wm. Bolthouse Farms, Inc.

OPPORTUNITY

Farming has evolved over the years into a very large business. The inputs into the farm can be quite expensive and can result in higher cost for the grower as well as the consumer. Bolthouse Farms determined that there was ample opportunity to reduce use of fossil fuels and conserve inputs such as water and pesticides to the farms.

SOLUTION

Solutions implemented by Bolthouse Farms included:

- Solar power farming—use of solar panels to generate energy

- Pivot irrigation
- Geographical Information System (GIS) precision farming
- Soil depletion prevention
- Spray Safe pesticide program
- Fresh Logistics rail freight forwarding
- Recyclable packaging

RESULTS

- Solar power farming reduced emissions and fossil fuel use.
- Solar panels generate energy for powering the pumps used to water the fields and the motors used in pivot irrigation.
- Pivot irrigation results in 20% less water used than in previous irrigation methods.
- Pivot irrigation reduces the use of pipe tractors, which lowers fuel use and emissions.
- Precision farming, which implements the use of a Geographic Information System (GIS), improves agricultural output while reducing the use of natural resources, thus reducing the farming "footprint" on the land.
- Soil depletion prevention, which is accomplished using harvesters that reduce the amount of dirt hauled into the plant by 3–5%, thereby reducing soil depletion.
- The Spray Safe program reduces pesticide usage and prevents pesticide drift incidents, which can harm nearby people and crops.
- Fresh Logistics distributes fresh produce via high-speed rail from Bakersfield to Chicago. It's a cleaner distribution

model that reduces CO2 emissions by millions of pounds and diesel fuel by hundreds of gallons.

- Beverage and salad dressing containers use PET #1 recyclable, a portion of which is made with regrind plastic. Carrot bag film is LDPE #4 recyclable. This reduces landfill waste.

Bioswales Remove Pollution from Surface Water Runoff

New Seasons Market

OPPORTUNITY

New Seasons was well into the development of its fifth store when a representative of the local neighborhood association approached it with an environmental concern—storm water runoff. Besides polluting rivers and streams, runoff after rain causes flooding and erosion, destroying habitats and contributing to sewer overflows.

At the time, plans for the new store included 15,000 square feet of non-permeable surfaces, which would mean another million gallons of storm water flowing out into the Willamette River. The company learned that Portland's Environmental Services had grant money available for businesses interested in implementing stormwater controls. By creating bioswales (bioswales are landscape elements designed to help remove silt and pollution from surface runoff water), New Seasons could reduce the impact the building would have on the environment.

SOLUTION

Although the project was already well underway and making modifications would likely increase costs and cause a delay in opening the new store, New Seasons decided to add a bioswale to its plans. The process included:

- Amending and obtaining approval for revised architectural plans
- Applying for new permits
- Applying for the grant to offset the costs

Much to New Seasons' surprise, once common ground was established among all the entities, things began to happen quickly. New plans were drawn up and submitted, the city granted New Seasons $50,000 for the bioswale, and the permits were hand carried by city employees between departments to speed up the process. The new store—with a bioswale—opened on time.

RESULTS

Today New Seasons has bioswales at seven of its twelve stores, which cycle over four million gallons of rainwater annually. The company benefits by reducing its environmental impact and an increased reputation as a sustainable business.

For more information, read *Growing Local Value: How to Build Business Partnerships That Strengthen Your Community* by Laury Hammel and Gun Denhart.

Composting and Recycle Sorting Reduce Waste and Disposal Costs

Standing Stone Brewing Company

OPPORTUNITY

Standing Stone Brewing Company has always encouraged employees to share their ideas and suggestions. Adopting green practices in more recent years has given Standing Stone the opportunity to engage its employees in new and previously unforeseen ways.

A server in the on-site restaurant observed the company's day-to-day operations and saw opportunities to reduce Standing Stone's overall waste.

SOLUTION

The employee proposed new practices, including composting and recycle sorting, to reduce overall waste and environmental impacts.

RESULTS

A year after these low-cost practices were adopted, overall waste has decreased by 95%, reducing the company's waste removal expenses by $2,400 annually.

Recycling and Recovery Reduce Waste Disposal Fees and Generate Revenue

Sierra Nevada Brewing Co.

OPPORTUNITY

Waste disposal fees are typically seen as a necessity for a business and something that cannot be avoided. However, what many fail to realize is that the materials that are being thrown away are resources that should and need to be recovered for beneficial reuse and recycling.

SOLUTION

Sierra Nevada Brewing Co. has established a world-class recycling and resource recovery program to keep materials from ending up in a landfill. Cardboard, shrink-wrap, cans, bottles, glass, scrap metal, paper, batteries, light bulbs, used motor oil, and food scraps are just some of the materials that are sorted out of the trash and recycled.

RESULTS

Through creative programs and partnerships, Sierra Nevada successfully diverts 99.8% of its total solid waste from landfill. Only 0.2% of the total discards generated by the entire facility are sent to a landfill.

Recycling programs are inexpensive to establish, returns are often almost immediate, and a revenue stream can be realized Sierra Nevada avoids more than $5 million on disposal fees while bringing in more than $860,000 in revenue by selling recovered materials. There are also significant greenhouse gas emission re-ductions associated with recycling as well as reduced energy and water consumption when manufacturing with recycled materials instead of virgin materials.

Reusable and Returnable Bags Reduce Paper Waste

Western Polymer Corporation

OPPORTUNITY

Western Polymer Corporation recovers starch from French fry and potato chip processing water before it enters the waste stream and modifies it for use in the paper industry.

The company originally packaged its starch products in 50-pound paper bags. All paper bags became waste at Western Polymer's plant or at its customers' locations and the company wanted a way to reduce this waste.

SOLUTION

To reduce the amount of waste paper, Western Polymer implemented the use of reusable, returnable bulk bags rather than disposable paper bags. Over the course of 15 years, the company was able to switch most customers to reusable bulk bags. The bulk bags are returned to Western Polymer and reused multiple times. When worn out, they are shipped to a recycler, completely avoiding landfill disposal.

RESULTS

This program has eliminated 364,000 pounds of paper waste per year.

In addition, the company added mechanical handling equipment to enable hydrated lime for the starch manufacturing process to be delivered and utilized with reusable bulk bags rather than 50-pound paper bags. This change eliminated 8,750 pounds of paper waste per year and reduced employees' exposure to hydrated lime by not having to physically handle the 50-pound paper bags.

Composting Reduces Waste and Landfill Costs

New Seasons Market

OPPORTUNITY

Since its founding in 2000, New Seasons Market has been committed to sustainable practices. In 2003, the company began separating organics for composting at all of its stores. New Seasons knew it could do more, so it enlisted the help of Portland Composts!, a Portland Bureau of Planning and Sustainability Initiative, in 2007.

SOLUTION

The program that was developed is called "Waste to Worth" and has three main components:

- Each of the 12 New Seasons stores targets the departments with the most waste.

- Color-coded containers—consistent across stores—are placed at points of high waste generation.
- Customized signage and training materials match both the waste guidance materials and the company's branding.

RESULTS

Every New Seasons store recycles and composts, resulting in a 50% reduction in overall garbage and conversion of 2,140 tons of organic waste to compost annually. Overall, composting saves New Seasons Market 30% compared to landfill costs, which amounted to more than $25,000 in 2011.

HotRot Composter Reduces Organic Waste and Produces Soil Amendments for Agriculural Application

Sierra Nevada Brewing Company

OPPORTUNITY

When organics are sent to a landfill instead of being composted, they produce methane as they break down. Methane is roughly 21 times more potent as a greenhouse gas than carbon dioxide, and food scraps in landfills are a primary source of methane. Chico, California, is located at the northern end of the Sacramento Valley and is in a fairly rural community. There are minimal composting outlets for the communities in the region and no food scrap composting options.

SOLUTION

Sierra Nevada Brewing Company encouraged the local community to pursue a regional food scraps composting facility. When encouragement resulted in no action, Sierra Nevada decided to purchase its own composting system. In 2010, Sierra Nevada purchased the country's first HotRot composting system to handle all of the brewery's spent food scraps and some spent brewing ingredients. The HotRot is capable of composting 4,000 pounds of organic material daily and produces a stable, nutrient-rich soil amendment that is used in onsite agricultural activities.

RESULTS

The brewery is composting all food scraps from its restaurant, concert venue, and break rooms (pre- and post-consumer), paper towels, hops from its dry hopping process, spent grain that is screened out of the wastewater effluent stream, and miscellaneous landscaping debris.

The HotRot composting system exemplifies an excellent closed-loop system where discards from the restaurant are turned into compost, which is used on the field that grows produce for the restaurant, which then creates the scraps that go right back out to the field. The system cost approximately $450,000.

Benefits from the system include reduced waste disposal fees, reduced greenhouse gas emissions, nutrient-rich soil amendment for use in onsite agricultural activities, opportunities to educate employees and consumers on important waste diversion practices, and a great story to tell.

Rail Transfer Facility Allows Greater Use of More Efficient and Cleaner Rail Transportation

Sierra Nevada Brewing Company

OPPORTUNITY

Transportation has arguably the most damaging environmental impacts in all of Sierra Nevada Brewing Company's operations, but it is something that is required in order for the company to sell its beers. Sierra Nevada recognizes that it will not entirely escape the negative impacts of transportation, but also knows that there are some very important things the company can do to reduce those impacts.

SOLUTION

In 2009, Sierra Nevada completed construction of a malt transfer facility just two miles from its plant. The facility includes more than two miles of rail track that come off of the main rail line that runs through Chico, as well as equipment to transfer malt from rail cars and into truck trailers.

Sierra Nevada is also shipping finished product via intermodal transportation. Intermodal transportation means that a truck trailer is filled with product at the brewery and driven by truck to the closest rail transfer facility. Trailers are loaded onto the train and railed across the United States instead of being trucked. More than 70% of Sierra Nevada's East Coast shipments arrive via rail.

RESULTS

Rail is an incredibly efficient and cost-effective way to move materials. Sierra Nevada now receives approximately 95% of its malt through the transfer facility. There are between three to four truckloads of malt in one rail car and multiple rail cars on each train, increasing the efficiency. Rail is 50% cleaner than traditional over-the-road truck travel. Benefits include reduced cost, increased efficiency, reduced fossil fuel use, and reduced greenhouse gas emissions. Sierra Nevada spent more than $1 million on the transfer facility, but it paid for itself in less than two years.

Smart Commuter Helps Employees Reduce Their Carbon Footprints

Bellingham Cold Storage

OPPORTUNITY

Bellingham Cold Storage (BCS) continuously seeks ways to lower its environmental footprint. BCS saw an opportunity to encourage employees to reduce their own carbon footprints.

SOLUTION

BCS established the SMART Commuter Program, which incentivizes employees to find alternatives to single-occupancy vehicles in their commute to work. BCS added a commuter checkbox on the daily timesheet to make it easy for BCS employees to report their SMART trips and for the company to track the success of the program.

RESULTS

On any given day, over a third of BCS employees carpool, bike, bus, or walk to work.

SMART Commuter increased BCS's reputation as a great employer and as a company focused on sustainability. It was recognized by the Environmental Protection Agency as one of the "Best Workplaces for Commuters" and has twice won the State of Washington's Governor's Award for innovation in workplace commuting.

Corporate social responsibility practices improve employee commitment and level of engagement to their core job function and to the company.[1] Research suggests that involvement in the company's corporate responsibility practices teaches workers valuable new skills that they bring back to their regular roles in the company.

---

1   Jeanne Meister, "Corporate Social Responsibility: A Lever for Employee Attraction & Engagement," *Forbes*, June 7, 2012, http://www.forbes.com/sites/jeannemeister/2012/06/07/corporate-social-responsibility-a-lever-for-employee-attraction-engagement/.

Green Machine Program Encourages Employees to Bike to Work

Sierra Nevada Brewing Co.

OPPORTUNITY

Sierra Nevada Brewing Co. continuously looks for ways to lower the carbon imprint of the company and its employees. One way was to create an incentive program that would encourage and reward employees to use their bicycles as a form of transportation.

SOLUTION

Through Sierra Nevada's Green Machine program, employees can pledge to ride their bikes to work, to run errands, or for regular recreation. Every three months, employees who met their pledges are entered into a drawing for gift certificates to local bike shops, and every May during Bike Week, bikes are given to two employees who met their pledges for the entire year.

Employees are also encouraged to take advantage of the Federal Bicycle Commuter Act benefit. This benefit provides an allowance of up to $20 per month to employees who ride their bikes to work at least more than half of their regularly scheduled shifts. The allowance can be used for reasonable expenses incurred in conjunction with riding to work, such as fixing the seat, breaks, light, bell, etc.

RESULTS

The Green Machine program has been highly successful for the past four years, and participation continues to increase.

Sonic Air Dryers More Energy Efficient than Compressed Air Dryers

Seneca Foods Corporation

OPPORTUNITY

Compressed air was used to remove water from cans on the production line before can coders marked the cans with numbers and text. This required energy to produce and maintain air pressure.

SOLUTION

The company replaced compressed air dryers with sonic air dryers. Sonic air dryers can perform the same water removal function but eliminate the need for high-energy use compressed air dryers. Seneca Foods Corporation had prior success with sonic dryers in the same application and had several sonic dryers left over from previous conversions in other areas.

RESULTS

The replacement saved the difference in cost between running the sonic dryers and operating the compressed air dryers. Eliminating the continuous use of compressed air through a ¼-inch airline reduced electrical energy consumption by 186,000 kilowatt-hours (kWh) per year at a cost savings of $9,300 per year.

Energy Efficiency Results in Stable Energy Costs Even with Increased Production

Sierra Nevada Brewing Co.

OPPORTUNITY

One can generate all the green power in the world one wants to, but if that power is not used efficiently, the purpose has been defeated. This rings true at Sierra Nevada Brewing Co., and the company has taken numerous steps to increase the energy efficiency of not only its equipment but of processes and employee behavior.

SOLUTION

Sierra Nevada has implemented the following energy efficiency measures:

- Tracking of electricity consumption
  - Tracking allows the user to notice and react quicker if there is something wrong in the process that is using more energy than it should. It also allows for the identification of positive trends in order to make sure they are continued.
- Retrofit of lighting fixtures and control systems
- Automation of equipment and processes
- Variable frequency drives on motors and pumps
- Increased water conservation
  - Water use, especially at a brewery, requires ample energy to move, treat, and use. When water is conserved, the energy that goes into its use is also conserved.

RESULTS

Sierra Nevada has been able to drive its kWh per barrel intensity down consistently over the last five years, resulting in stable energy costs despite the fact that production has increased. Cost savings and optimized utilization of onsite electricity generation technologies. Some projects are more cost-intensive than others, but most do not involve a cost at all, simply a change in the way something is done.

Lighting Retrofit of Old System Reduces Energy Costs

Del Monte Foods

OPPORTUNITY

Del Monte Foods continuously seeks ways to reduce cost and energy consumption. Looking for ways to reduce energy use, the Yakima plant team determined that the best option was to reduce energy consumption in the old, outdated lighting system.

SOLUTION

The team proposed a lighting retrofit project to replace 100% of internal plant lighting with modern T8 fixtures and lamps. In order to pay for the $140,000 project, the Yakima team applied for two grants, which provided a total of $88,000 to the plant to help fund this project, reducing Del Monte's total cost for this project to $52,000.

RESULTS

The ongoing annual savings of 538,000 kWh produces cost savings of $25,000 per year for a return on investment in just over two years including the grant (and less than six years if the grant isn't considered).

Solar Power Reduces Demand Charges and Supplies Part of Power Needs

Sierra Nevada Brewing Co.

OPPORTUNITY

Sierra Nevada Brewing Co. relies on the local power grid for electricity. There are a number of problems when relying on such a grid. First, there are frequent power outages as the grid attempts to keep up with demand. When Sierra Nevada loses power, there is the potential to lose product, which results in lost resources and money. Additionally, the local utility grid depends heavily on fossil fuel consumption in order to produce the needed electricity. To reduce environmental impacts, looking for alternative sources of renewable electricity is essential.

SOLUTION

In 2010, Sierra Nevada Brewing Co. completed what is now one of the largest privately owned solar installations in the country. Solar photovoltaic electricity is a clean and 100% renewable source of electricity. Sierra Nevada's solar system covers a three-acre parking lot as well as all available roof space. Sierra Nevada's onsite daycare facility and rail facility are also 100% solar powered.

RESULTS

All together, Sierra Nevada's solar systems are capable of producing 2 megawatts of direct current (DC) electricity and include over 10,000 individual photovoltaic panels. In 2011, the solar system produced 2,596,545 kWh, or 18% of Sierra Nevada's total electricity needs—roughly equivalent to powering 261 average American households. Solar panels are ideal for utility customers that are on a time-of-use rate structure and have demand charges. Because solar panels work during the heat of the day, demand charges are dramatically reduced, resulting in much lower utility bills. Sierra Nevada's solar system saves the company more than $100,000 annually.

Solar panels will obviously reduce a company's utility costs, but there are a number of other peripheral benefits to utilizing solar. Investing in alternative energy ensures a more stable source of power for future years, demonstrates corporate citizenship and environmental stewardship, reduces the company environmental footprint, and builds a culture that employees are happy to be a part of.

Sierra Nevada spent roughly $2 million out-of-pocket for the solar systems. This was after the many state and federal rebates and incentives the company received for installing the system.

For more information, see http://www.sierranevada.com/environment/solar.html.

Energy Efficient Air Compressor Project Produces Significant Energy Savings

Seneca Foods Corporation

OPPORTUNITY

A Seneca Foods Corporation facility had an antiquated, poorly working air system that ran a can dryer.

The company engaged its local equipment maintenance vendor to analyze the air system and identify options to improve operating efficiency.

SOLUTION

Efficiency improvements included installing one new compressor with a variable frequency drive and a new dryer. The company also installed a new 5,000-gallon air holding tank to help handle the demand surges from the retorts (sterilization process).

RESULTS

The total cost of the project was approximately $100,000, but energy conservation incentives from the electrical utility would offset some of the cost once the savings were verified. Overall, after verification by the equipment maintenance vendor, the improvements to the air system reduced the facility's energy consumption by 440,000 kilowatt-hours per year. The electric utility company issued incentives of approximately $53,000, bringing the net capital cost to $47,000. Seneca Foods saves $22,000 per year in electricity costs and now has updated equipment that works.

Hydrogen Fuel Cells for Electric Generation

Sierra Nevada Brewing Co.

OPPORTUNITY

Sierra Nevada Brewing Co. relies on the local power grid for electricity. There are a number of problems when relying on such a grid. First, there are frequent power outages as the grid attempts to keep up with demand. When Sierra Nevada loses power, there is the potential to lose product, which results in lost resources and money. Additionally, the local utility grid depends heavily on fossil fuel consumption in order to produce the needed electricity. To reduce environmental impacts, looking for alternative sources of renewable electricity is essential.

SOLUTION

For these reasons, Sierra Nevada began looking for clean alternatives to grid-supplied electricity and in 2005 became the first brewing operation in the United States to install hydrogen fuel cells. The onsite facility consists of four 250 kW fuel cell energy units that together are capable of generating 1 megawatt of direct current electricity. The fuel cells run on natural gas and generate a consistent supply of electricity to Sierra Nevada operations. To enhance the fuel cells' efficiency, heat recovery units were added to recover the 950°F exhaust leaving the units and to produce steam that is recycled back into the brewing process.

RESULTS

In 2011, the fuel cells produced 6,158,838 kWh, or 43% of electricity needs—roughly equivalent to powering 620 average American households. The heat recovery units add 15% efficiency to the installation. After state and federal rebates, grants, and incentives, the out-of-pocket costs were between $2–2.5 million on the project—roughly 70% of the total installation costs were covered.

Sierra Nevada has experienced reduced utility bills including lower demand charges, established the company as a leader in corporate citizenship and environmental stewardship, and helped an emerging technology take shape.

PART THREE

ECONOMIC SUSTAINABILITY

Economic Sustainability is the development of innovative business opportunities, services, and products that produce positive company image and recognition.

—*Northwest Food Processors Sustainability Guide*

INTRODUCING ECONOMIC SUSTAINABILITY

Economic sustainability assures that a company is viable for the long term by managing according to principles that support the environment and the community as well as the company's economic well-being. The sustainable company operates so that its employees, customers, partners, communities, and shareholders all benefit.

Shareholder/stakeholder value is an essential component to the longevity of a business. Incorporating sustainability into strategic planning and business practices can lead to better innovation, competitive advantage, access to new markets, and increased margins or market share.

Innovation is critical to sustaining any enterprise; those that do not innovate eventually disappear. Sustainable innovation seeks to produce new products, services, and processes while efficiently using materials, energy, and labor and reducing waste. In essence, innovation leads to increased productivity, which leads to increased competitiveness and increased profits.

Human capital protection is essential for employee morale and for accessing untapped creative potential. Sustainable companies recognize that employees are their most valuable asset. They understand the importance of encouragement and recognition for positive contributions and of engaging and maintaining a superior workforce.

Partnerships can be an important investment as a company seeks opportunities for economic sustainability. Product and service providers, educational institutions, consultants, government agencies, and non-governmental organizations can be a source of information, solutions, and problem solving. Investigate the resources in your industry cluster, and engage them to assist your company in achieving its sustainability goals.

ENERGY EFFICIENCY MAKES GOOD BUSINESS SENSE

Energy efficiency contributes to economic sustainability in the following ways:

- Energy affects the bottom line; it can be a company's single-largest *uncontrolled* expense.
- Energy efficiency mitigates the impacts of rising energy prices or volatile energy markets.
- Energy efficiency improves productivity, enhances reliability, and improves safety.
- Energy accounts for over 90% of greenhouse gas emissions.
- Incentives and technical assistance are available for energy efficiency projects and O&M.

Because of the importance of energy efficiency, in 2009, NWFPA adopted a goal to reduce industry-wide energy intensity by 25% in 10 years and 50% in 20 years. Access the NWFPA Energy Roadmap at **http://www.nwfpa.org** under Energy.

Questions to Ask

- Does my company actively seek development of new products and processes?
- Does my company have a plan for infrastructure improvement and process investment?
- Does my company have a program for employee engagement, skills training and development, and recognition of contributions?
- What hidden resources, and hidden liabilities, does my company have/
- What potential partners could bring valuable resources to assist our efforts?

Employee-Driven Continuous Improvement

Bellingham Cold Storage

OPPORTUNITY

In 2000, Doug Thomas, Bellingham Cold Storage's president and CEO, started Excellence through Continuous Improvement (ECI), a program that engaged employees in decisions and process improvement at all levels of the organization. An expanded ECI program would further improve productivity, efficiency, and accuracy.

SOLUTION

Bellingham Cold Storage (BCS) implemented Kaizen, an agile and rapid technique to identify processes that seem redundant, require unnecessary hard work, or can be improved to make employee jobs safer and/or more efficient. Kaizen is a Japanese philosophy of continuous improvement of processes in business, management, engineering, and manufacturing. Kaizen (改善) means "change for the better."

Employees place their suggestions for process improvement on Kaizen boards, which are located throughout the plant in the various production areas. Through a team-based process, employees decide whether to implement each suggestion. After teams are assigned to a course of action to implement the suggestion, it is moved from the suggestion side of the Kaizen board to the solution side, which indicates that it is now part of the work routine. When a solution has been fully implemented, it is taken off the board and added to a running list of actions that is renewed every year.

Employees can make as many suggestions as they want. For each idea submitted, employees receive a small cash reward in their paycheck, providing an immediate incentive for sharing ideas. The amount of the cash award is determined based upon the amount of savings to the company that is produced by the idea. Additionally, each year one employee receives an award for having the most Kaizen ideas that year.

RESULTS

BCS has saved almost $250,000 since Kaizen was implemented and has awarded almost $10,000 in cash awards to employees. Employee engagement and satisfaction have increased and quality and productivity have improved as well as company profits.

Community-based On-Site Ammonia Safety Training

Bellingham Cold Storage

OPPORTUNITY

For Bellingham Cold Storage (BCS), the safety of its community comes first. The company is committed to ensuring that anyone who handles anhydrous ammonia knows how to handle and store it properly. Training is required, but the Ammonia Safety Training Institute is located in Watsonville, California and traveling and attendance is cost prohibitive for smaller companies that work with anhydrous ammonia. BCS saw an opportunity to make its community safer by making training more accessible.

SOLUTION

Many companies would not allow competitors on their work-sites, but BCS invites any company, including its competitors, working with anhydrous ammonia to attend its safety training. BCS's tenants, fire departments, and any business in Whatcom and Skagit Counties that meets the legal threshold for required training is invited.

RESULTS

Fire departments and company on-site emergency responders are trained side-by-side before an emergency, which helps with communication and flow during a crisis. A side benefit is the intercompany and community relationships that are formed during the training.

Employee Workforce Referral Pipeline

Green Mountain Coffee Roasters, Inc.

OPPORTUNITY

The workforce at Green Mountain Coffee Roaster's Sumner plant more than tripled over a two-year period and is expected to grow by more than 60% within the next two years. A pipeline of highly qualified workers was needed to fill these positions.

SOLUTION

Employees were encouraged to refer prospective employees to the company by the award of a cash bonus when a new hire that they had referred satisfactorily reaches the six-month employment milestone.

RESULTS

Green Mountain is able to tap into the employees' "circle of influence" to build a robust referral pipeline and reduce recruitment costs. Frontline workers are motivated to only refer the best candidates and feel they are contributing to the long-term success of the company.

Communicating the Vision to Employees

Dave's Killer Bread

OPPORTUNITY

Dave's Killer Bread has cultivated a loyal workforce and regularly looks for ways to improve employee satisfaction and morale. An employee survey revealed a desire for more communication between frontline workers and supervisors. The company sought to create a better system to communicate the company vision and direction and encourage employees to share their ideas and suggestions.

SOLUTION

Dave's Killer Bread management initiated quarterly company meetings for each shift. The meetings set context for the company and are structured as questions and answers for employees. Employees are also given time to share their opinions and suggestions for improvements.

In addition, supervisors hold five-minute standing meetings before each shift to set context for the day and to make announcements.

RESULTS
Employees are more committed to the company's overall success because they know and understand how they fit into the overall strategic direction of the company. Standing meetings give employees the opportunity to ask questions, provide feedback, and get issues addressed in real-time, which positively impacts their productivity and quality of work.

Financial Literacy Program Reduces Employee Stress

Green Mountain Coffee Roasters, Inc.

OPPORTUNITY

Green Mountain Coffee Roasters has always been committed to its employee's financial success. Employees can participate in an employee stock purchase plan (ESPP) where they buy company stock at a 15% discounted price through payroll deductions. The company automatically enrolls employees in a 401(k) program in which the company offers a 50% match of the employee contribution up to the 6% maximum deduction.

During the 2000s, the average US employee experienced increased financial stress due to the dramatic increase in home foreclosures and defaults on credit cards. The Federal Reserve has calculated that the average employee spends 28 hours each month worried about, calculating, or stressed over finances, costing employers $5,000 a year per employee in lost productivity.[2]

Green Mountain knew the economic crisis was having an impact on its employees, potentially draining productivity and increasing emotional stress on the job. Green Mountain saw an opportunity to help employees gain financial literacy to meet their short- and long-term financial goals by addressing their financial concerns.

SOLUTION

Employees can enroll in a financial literacy program called Dave Ramsey's Financial Peace University. This program teaches employees and their families how to make the right decisions to achieve financial goals and experience a total money makeover to become debt-free.

RESULTS

When employees feel secure about their personal finances, they are less stressed and so are more productive, happier, healthier, and miss fewer days of work.

Note: Learn more about Dave Ramsey's Financial Peace University at http://www.daveramsey.com.

---

2 "Employee Financial Education," National Financial Educators Council, http://www.financialeducatorscouncil.org/employee-financial-education.html.

A Living Wage for All Employees Boosts Productivity

Dave's Killer Bread

OPPORTUNITY

Frontline workers are challenged to find a job that pays more than minimum wage. Dave's Killer Bread saw an opportunity to create a pay system that was more equitable for all employees.

SOLUTION

Dave's Killer Bread eliminated its annual bonus program and increased all employees' pay to a living wage.

RESULTS

Paying employees a living wage gives them dignity, as they are able to afford basic necessities, without public or private assistance. It decreases financial stress, which improves employee productivity, work quality and morale and reduces absenteeism.

Incentives for Growers to be More Sustainable

Sierra Nevada Brewing Co.

OPPORTUNITY

High-quality beer requires high-quality ingredients, which depend upon a healthy environment. Sierra Nevada uses only non–genetically modified barley, which has a lower protein content, and hops that have been bred using traditional methods. Lower protein content increases the amount of fermentable sugar available to the brewer, which means a more efficient use of grain. The company also wanted to encourage its barley farmers to incorporate more sustainable farming practices.

SOLUTION

The company launched a new program called "Farm with Your Brewer" to partner with growers on production strategies that target lower-protein barley and are more sustainable. In order to participate in the program, farmers must do the following:

- Switch to notill production.
- Change planting and spray applications to minimize the use of fertilizer and chemicals.
- Analyze the soil throughout the field to insure that the correct amount of fertilizer is applied.
- Use a Global Positioning System (GPS) in their operation to reduce fuel consumption and chemical applications.
- Reduce transportation impacts by growing barley within a 40-mile radius of the Prairie Malt Facility or must ensure that trucks make a return trip loaded with another commodity.
- Complete an Environmental Farm Plan (EFP) for their operation.
- Be a prairie steward and adhere to the Saskatchewan Soil Conservation Association (SSCA) Code of Conservation Ethics as well as become a member of the SSCA.

When a grower agrees to the above practices, Sierra Nevada pays a financial incentive up front to offset the risk faced by changing practices. The grower keeps the incentive whether or not he or she meets the protein specifications. If the protein requirements are met, the grower receives an additional premium price for the barley.

RESULTS

Four growers have signed on for the threeyear pilot project.

Partner with State Employment Training to Reduce Training Costs and Increase Employee Skills

Sierra Nevada Brewing Co.

OPPORTUNITY

Sierra Nevada Brewing Co.'s growth rates had accelerated over previous years, and with the growing demand, the company experienced a greater need for qualified and technically trained employees to support additional production demands.

SOLUTION

Sierra Nevada worked with the State of California's Employment Training Panel (ETP). This partnership offset the costs of job skills training necessary to maintain a high-performance workplace and strengthen the company's competitive edge. Sierra Nevada now trains its employees in commercial, business, hazardous materials, and management skills. Training is done in conjunction with other departments in two-hour increments.

RESULTS

Training has resulted in a better-skilled workforce, increased employee satisfaction and loyalty and lower turnover. Cross-departmental training ensures that employees get to know each other and gain a better understanding of the entire production line, including brewing, bottling, tours, and restaurant operations.

Employee Training Improves Productivity and Employee Retention

Tim's Cascade Chips

OPPORTUNITY

Over the years Tim's Cascade Chips has gone through numerous major acquisitions; most recently, Pinnacle Foods acquired Tim's in 2009. Amidst the natural turmoil caused by significant company changes, Tim's knows it needs to retain its experienced and skilled frontline workers to keep up with increasing demands on productivity and consistently produce the unique kettle-style chips and quality snacks for which Tim's has become famous.

SOLUTION

Tim's gives employees in-depth on-the-job training and also cross-trains them in several positions. For specialized training, Tim's employees can now participate in one of Pinnacle Foods' online learning programs called "Reach Your Peak," which is a suite of learning tools to help employees further develop their knowledge and achieve personal performance goals. To participate, employees and managers co-develop a learning plan using a competency development guide, which helps managers track the professional development of their staff. Employees have continuous opportunities to improve their skills by taking advantage of new opportunities, such as assisting in training new hires or delivering quarterly trainings for all employees.

RESULTS

Production is steadily growing between 10 to 15% per year, and accidents have decreased by 9.4% over a five-year period. Cross-training ensures that Tim's maintains high quality and predictable output per hour, as employees are able to work on different production lines.

Mechanical Separation of Packaging from Food Wastes allows Recycling and Eliminates Disposal Fees.

Pacific Natural Foods

OPPORTUNITY

Pacific Natural Foods, a producer of all natural and organic foods, adopted a goal of zero waste to landfill, where discard materials are minimized or reused and all remaining wastes are recycled or composted. In 2006, Pacific Natural Foods adopted recycling rate as a key performance indicator and by 2007, it was recovering 40% of its wastes.

However, much of the waste going to landfill went via a large, highly visible, and messy compactor that took waste from the production lines. A waste sort conducted by Portland State University's Community Environmental Services revealed that 95% of this waste was food-contaminated packaging material. Manually separating the product from the packaging was cost-prohibitive, so all of this waste—50 tons or more in a typical month—went to landfill.

THE SOLUTION

Pacific Natural Foods designed and constructed, at a cost of over $100,000, a customized "de-packing" station that mechanically separates the unsellable product from the packaging. This eliminated a considerable flow of waste to the landfill. Packaging materials are now being recycled and Pacific Natural Foods is exploring options to divert the food residuals to anaerobic digestion or other beneficial uses.

BENEFITS

The company's recycling rate jumped from 40% in 2007 to 88% in August 2011, the month Pacific Natural Foods "retired" its garbage compactor (complete with a retirement party, as featured in this funny spoof of The Office: please see http://www.youtube.com/watch?v=A9T05pkAErg). In 2012, the recycling operation saved over $100,000 in disposal fees and generated approximately $65,000 in revenue—financial benefits that help to justify the full-time employment of four recycling specialists.

In-sourcing Ingredients Improves Quality and Engages Employees

Standing Stone Brewing Company

OPPORTUNITY

Since its founding, Standing Stone Brewing Company has looked for ways to operate its brewery and restaurant that protect and restore the environment and support the health and happiness of its community, guests, and employees. In addition to sourcing its ingredients as locally as possible, Standing Stone saw an opportunity to "insource" its ingredients from its own farming operations and engage its employees in new and unforeseen ways.

SOLUTION

In 2011, the company leased nearby farmland and is now producing its own eggs and beef as well as raising other animals on the farm. Rather than hiring a professional farmer, Standing Stone asked a neighboring farmer to help train the company's staff. A rotating handful of employees now work at the farm in the early morning hours composting, feeding chickens and cows, moving fences, and collecting eggs for the restaurant.

RESULTS

The company has seen reduced costs and improved product quality. In addition, the enthusiasm that Standing Stone employees gain from helping to bring organic food from the farm directly onto customers' plates often spills over into conversations with customers, which is great publicity for the company.

Onsite Agriculture Supplies Quality and Sustainable Raw Materials

Sierra Nevada Brewing Co.

OPPORTUNITY

Beer is made of four primary ingredients: barley, hops, yeast, and water. Because Sierra Nevada Brewing Co. relies so heavily on agricultural products, the company was interested to learn as much as possible about the crops used as well as some of the barriers to moving toward more sustainable farming practices. Sierra Nevada also has a very successful onsite restaurant that is one of the most popular restaurants in Chico, California. The company strives to serve the most fresh, local, and organic ingredients possible—and how much closer can you get than onsite?

SOLUTION

Sierra Nevada maintains an eight-acre hop field and a two-acre garden for the restaurant on the brewery property in Chico. The company also has a thirty-acre barley field located at its rail facility just two miles from the brewery. All of these fields are certified organic by Oregon Tilth.

RESULTS

The hop and barley fields are harvested and used to brew Sierra Nevada's Estate Harvest Ale. This beer is the company's only certified organic beer and is made with ingredients straight from its fields. The restaurant garden yields year-round produce and herbs that are as fresh as they could possibly be. These fields also receive compost that is made onsite from discarded food and other organic discards from the brewing process, creating an elegant closed-loop program.

Employees learn about farming practices and have a greater connection and appreciation for the farmers that supply raw materials. This creates a fantastic story for consumers.

Biodiesel from Spent Vegetable Oil Offsets Petroleum Fuels Use

Sierra Nevada Brewing Co.

OPPORTUNITY

One of the guiding sustainability approaches at Sierra Nevada Brewing Co. is to close resource loops whenever possible. This requires the brewery to look at what is leaving its facility and what is coming in. The goal is to recover resources that are leaving and find a way to bring them back into plant operations. One of these resources that was leaving was used vegetable oil from the onsite restaurant. One of the resources that is consumed is fuel for the company's fleet.

SOLUTION

In 2008, Sierra Nevada investigated biodiesel production using the spent vegetable oil from its restaurant. The brewery purchased a BioPro 190 biodiesel processor in February of that year and began biodiesel production. The processor is capable of handling 50-gallon batches of used vegetable oil and processing it into biodiesel in 48 hours. Sierra Nevada's restaurant produces roughly 50 gallons of spent vegetable oil every week and the machine is able to process the restaurant's entire output. Sierra Nevada paid $9,000 for the machine and received a $1,000 tax credit. The machine paid for itself in about 18 months and the biodiesel now costs the company about $1.80 per gallon. The finished biodiesel is used in Sierra Nevada's fleet of trucks to offset petroleum fuel consumption.

RESULTS

Since purchasing the machine, Sierra Nevada has processed 7,500 gallons of spent vegetable oil into alternative fuel. Reduced greenhouse gas emissions, reduced dependence on petroleum fuel, avoided disposal costs of spent vegetable oil, job/task creation, and a wonderful closed-loop story to share with consumers are all benefits of this activity.

On-site Electric Vehicle Charging Stations

Sierra Nevada Brewing Co.

OPPORTUNITY

In early 2009, Sierra Nevada Brewing Co. was approached by a local electric car dealer asking if the company would install electric vehicle charging stations. Sierra Nevada owner Ken Grossman knew that if technology like electric vehicles is going to be feasible, the infrastructure for those technologies needs to be in place. For this reason, Ken agreed to install charging stations, hoping it would help the technology catch on in the Chico, California community.

SOLUTION

Sierra Nevada installed two Coloumb electric vehicle charging stations in its public parking lot in April 2009. The electric car dealership went out of business shortly after the chargers were installed, and there were no electric vehicles in Chico to speak of. The chargers are tied directly to Sierra Nevada's solar array that covers the parking lot where vehicles can be charged using a renewable source of electricity. The chargers at the facility are offered free to anyone driving an electric vehicle to the brewery— employees, vendors, and guests. Sierra paid a total of $3,000 for the two chargers with network monitoring.

RESULTS

The chargers sat idle until 2011 when the Nissan Leaf came on the market. The chargers are still not getting as much attention as the brewery would have hoped—in fact, their only regular use is for two company-owned electric vehicles! Sierra Nevada is at the very least prepared for the future demand.

The installation of the charging station shows company commitment to the future, promotes the use of alternative fuel, encourages reduction in petroleum consumption, and improves customer relations.

Green Teams Drive Recycling Program Successes

New Seasons Market

OPPORTUNITY

In 2007, New Seasons implemented a highly successful recycling and composting program, called "Waste to Worth," in all of its groceries stores. New Seasons management knew that the success of the program was dependent upon employees' enthusiasm and passion for implementing sustainable practices and the ability to drive costs savings through the identification of waste-reducing best practices specific to each department.

SOLUTION

New Seasons piloted its first Green Team at one store by identifying a "green champion" and other store employees who believed their store could do better. The success of that pilot led company management to support and encourage expansion of the model to all store locations.

As in the pilot, the New Seasons sustainability manager and each store manager identified an employee or group of employees passionate about reducing their store's environmental impact and then built the Green Teams around their leadership.

Green Team Basics

- Each store must have a Green Team which includes at least one staff member from each department.
- Teams get up to 40 hours of paid time to choose a community service project each year.
- The teams meet for 30 to 60 minutes each month and are paid for that time.

RESULTS

Every New Seasons store recycles and composts, resulting in a 50% reduction in overall garbage and conversion of 2,140 tons of organic waste to compost. Composting saves New Seasons Market 30% compared to landfill costs, which amounted to more than $25,000 in 2011. The Green Teams have increased employee professional development and leadership opportunities and improved employee loyalty and satisfaction.